# A Way to Quit Gambling

# A Way to Quit Gambling

## (for problem gamblers)

*John Chin*

**Writer's Showcase presented by *Writer's Digest***
San Jose  New York  Lincoln  Shanghai

A Way to Quit Gambling
(for problem gamblers)

Published by Writer's Showcase presented by *Writer's Digest*
an imprint of iUniverse.com, Inc.


For information address:
iUniverse.com, Inc.
620 North 48th Street
Suite 201
Lincoln, NE 68504-3467
www.iuniverse.com


ISBN: 0-595-08868-6

Printed in the United States of America

# Dedication

This book is dedicated to the families of problem gamblers. They suffer greatly, as well.

# Contents

# Preface

Many terms are used to classify gamblers, such as occasional gamblers, social gamblers, casual gamblers, serious gamblers, compulsive gamblers, pathological gamblers, etc. However, there are basically two types of gamblers. There are those who can control their gambling and those who can not.

Gamblers who can control their gambling always know when to quit. Most of them break even, lose a little, or even win a little year after year. They have gambling under control and do not need help from anyone.

Gamblers who cannot control their gambling are problem gamblers. Gambling is a real problem in their lives. They gamble regularly and have significant overall losses every or nearly every year. The National Gambling Impact Study Commission estimates about 20 million adults in the USA to be or be capable of being problem gamblers. (1)

---

There has been little funded and effective help for problem gamblers. This is mainly because there is nothing visually wrong or infectious with them. Compared to those with serious health diseases, everyone is inclined to have less compassion and pity for problem gamblers. Even the $5 million National Impact Study Commission on Gambling (1997-1999) was far short on addressing and alleviating the plight of problem gamblers. So, I decided to make my notes and views organized into this manual available to help other problem gamblers get started on solving their problem.

The aim of this manual is to help hinder and stop problem gamblers from gambling and the downward financial and emotional spiral that they usually face. Problem gamblers who have already tried to quit unsuccessfully may find the points contained in this manual to echo many of their own thoughts. At the very least, this manual should point most problem gamblers in the right direction.

However, this manual can provide only limited help for those who gamble over their heads, lose more than they have, and have a negative net worth. These individuals should seek further help from Gamblers Anonymous (see Appendix B) and a gambling counselor. Furthermore, those who have engaged in illegal activities to raise cash for gambling need all of the help they can get and should consult both a gambling counselor and a psychiatrist. Wives of compulsive gamblers can contact Gam-Anon (see Appendix B).

# Acknowledgements

Many thanks to Michelle Shotkoski, Joyce Greenfield, Elizabeth vonRentzell and other staff members at iUniverse, who assisted me getting this book published.

I also wish to thank USA Today and the Poughkeepsie Journal for reporting on the National Gambling Impact Study Commission and the dire situation of problem gamblers. Without seeing this news, I would not have proceeded with this book.

# List of Abbreviations

OTB—Off Track Betting

vig—vigorish

# Introduction

Gambling changed my life. I was always fascinated with medical doctors, as a kid. When I was in seventh grade and only 12 years old, I started to dream of becoming a great medical research doctor. Like many mothers, my mom also wanted me to become a doctor when I grew up. However, my life and goal started to change when I was 18 and got involved with OTB.

Later, my gambling expanded to live night-time and weekend horse racing. All of my spare time during college was spent frequenting New York City OTB parlors, Aqueduct & Belmont turf racing tracks, and Roosevelt & Yonkers Raceways.

One night at Roosevelt, I bet my last $4 that I needed for a bus ride back home. I lost that bet and tried to beg the bus driver for a ride home. Fortunately, I was instructed to get a "CHIT" sheet from the Public Relations office. That night, I realized that I had a real problem in gambling and was possibly some kind of derelict.

Combining gambling with college study took its toll. My college grades were mostly B's & C's, when I had the ability to get mostly A's. I ended up downgrading my college aims and chose to major in computer science and mathematics as a sophomore, with hopes of landing a job right out of college. By that time, I lost all of my savings that mainly came from hard part-time work at my neighborhood pharmacy and summer work painting dormitory rooms.

In 1977, I got a steady computer programming job at a publishing company in New York and I started to save money again. However, a year later, casino gambling came to Atlantic City, New Jersey. Curiosity and the thought of winning money struck my mind again. Initially, I had outrageous "beginner's luck" and won often at blackjack and craps. It was unbelievable and I even had the thought that I could make a living gambling.

Luckily, I never quit my job because I eventually had my share of losses. In 1980, I made the first of many trips to Las Vegas, Reno/Lake Tahoe, and Robinsonville/Tunica. Later, I also dabbled in many other types of gambling, trying unsuccessfully to find one that I could consistently win at.

Over time, I suffered huge losses (relative to what I earned working and saved) as most problem gamblers do. There were a few years that I was in the red and gambled with money from credit cards. I tried to quit gambling dozen of times.

After more than a decade of spending the majority of my free time gambling, I really started to change by first buying a condominium and tying myself up with a mortgage. Then, I gradually imposed increasingly smaller limits on the amount of time and money that I would spend gambling, reducing my gambling by 90% over a decade. In 1998, I made what I hope is my last trip to Las Vegas and Reno/Lake Tahoe for gambling, using my last free round trip ticket from accumulated air miles.

After that, I started writing down all of my observations, thoughts, and ideas that I had whenever I tried to give up gambling. By finally putting this information into concrete form, I was able to easily review the information quickly and regularly. It has saved me from having to re-learn painful lessons over and over again. These notes have helped me to not make a bet in over a year, the longest span of time that I have not gambled.

# Section One

# The History and Future of Gambling

It is important to realize how big gambling really is and not to fault oneself for being a gambler. People who gamble a lot usually carry the negative stigma of being a gambler with family, relatives, friends, and co-workers. There is an inherent sinfulness in gambling, in terms of greed. However, realize that most people, whether they admit or not, have gambled money.

To break away from gambling, the problem gambler needs to know and understand all there is about gambling. Know the enemy. Gambling is here to stay. It is big business that is destined to become more prevalent in the future. It is up to the problem gambler to awaken and do something about his gambling problem.

# Chapter 1

# History of Gambling

## 1.1 Gambling's Long History

Gambling artifacts have been found in ancient China, India, and Egypt. (2) Ivory dice, dated before 1500 BC, were found at Thebes. (3) Gambling permeates nearly all societies. Now, there is legalized gambling in over 90 countries. Legalized gambling is as widespread as most other major industries.

## 1.2 Types of Gambling

In the USA, there are many ways to gamble including:

a) Pari-mutuel Betting, which includes Horse (Thoroughbred Turf & Standardbred Harness) Racing, OTB, Dog Racing, & Jai alai
b) Casino Table Games and Slots
c) Lottery, Bingo, Keno, and other random number games
d) Sports Bookmaking, which includes college and professional sports wagering

e) Illegal and inhumane Animal Fights like cock fighting and pit-bull matches

f) Poker, pan, bridge, gin & other types of rummy, cribbage and other card games

In addition, there are quasi-gambling tournaments for backgammon, chess, checkers, billiards, dart throwing, knife throwing, horseshoe throwing, bowling, golf, tennis, etc. Winners are awarded tournament prizes and there can be friendly betting between the contestants and among spectators.

## 1.3 Legalized Gambling

In the United States of America, gambling is big business, a multi-billion dollar annual industry. $300 billion was gambled in 1990 .(4) Casino revenues was about $16.5 billion in 1994 .(5) Overall, gambling revenues were $39.9 billion in 1994 (6) and almost $51 billion in 1997.

(7) Illegal gambling establishments and bookies have existed for ages. Because of their nature, they operated in secrecy from law enforcement and catered to a small private customer base. Over the past few decades, this customer base has shrunk because of ever increasing legalized gambling.

Prohibition does no good, as criminal elements simply step in with illegal gambling. Governments have been acknowledging this fact. It is better for governments to legalize gambling and use gambling revenues to fund social and educational programs. At least, in this manner, there is some good that comes out of gambling for society.

There are additional good points for legalized gambling. It employs many people, attracts tourism and generates phenomenal revenues for local communities. Let us also not forget that gambling is first and foremost legitimate entertainment to millions of people, who can handle it (by limiting the amount of money they gamble).

The trend is clearly toward more legalized gambling in the USA and other democratic societies. In the mid-1800's, gambling was legalized in Nevada as towns were growing, but was banned between 1910-1931. In the late 1800's, there was illegal horse race gambling. In 1908, there was pari-mutuel betting for the Kentucky Derby. In 1940, pari-mutuel betting started at Roosevelt Raceway in New York with standardbred harness racing. In 1970, OTB was legalized in New York City.

In 1978, casino gambling started in Atlantic City, New Jersey and since, has spread to many other states and countries. Some huge casino resort destinations include Las Vegas/Laughlin in Nevada, Reno/Lake Tahoe in Nevada, Atlantic City in New Jersey, and Tunica/Robinsonville in Mississippi.

There is also a new twist to legalized gambling in the USA with American Indian Casino Gaming. In 1998, there were about 200 American Indian casinos. They have spread like wild fire across America into non-resort areas that are usually surrounded by well-populated residential communities. These casinos make gambling available around the clock to more working families than ever.

With Indian casinos, there are now 26 states with casino gambling. In 1995, there was legalized gambling in every state, except Hawaii and Utah.

In many localities, Las Vegas Nights are sponsored by social organizations as fund raising activity. Most gambling revenues go to a good social cause. Odds are usually a little worse than at real casinos. However, low minimum and maximum bet limits are imposed, so that gamblers usually do not lose too much money during a night.

# Chapter 2

# Future of Gambling

## 2.1 Government Regulations

There has been much debate by individuals and various organizations for government to better regulate gambling. However, gambling advocates are better funded to win every debate.

Although US Federal and state governments may enact laws to limit legalized gambling in minor ways, there is no chance for them to ever eliminate it. Remember there are many good points for legalized gambling. These governments now have huge stakes in terms of tax revenues from legalized gambling. There is also little that can now be done to regulate American Indian gaming.

## 2.2 Advertising

Advertising is vital to legalized gambling establishments. However, they can advertise freely to the public and lure anyone, including problem gamblers and those who never would have engaged in illegal gambling activities. Free speech rights will ultimately allow legalized gambling establishments to advertise in a limited manner, if not freely to the general public. Any rules would be equivalent to those imposed on alcohol and tobacco advertising.

Most gambling establishments are already adept at advertising and are big on freebies. They use promotions, comps, or gimmicks to bring gamblers (esp. losers) back.

Amazingly, casinos award comps equal to about 40% of expected winnings from a player based on many averages (player's average size of bet x hours played x average number of bets per hour in the game being played x the casino percent advantage for the game being played). The top casinos in Las Vegas return about 11% of profits back to gamblers in the form of comps. People love to get something for nothing. However, they can end up paying or losing many times more money than these offers are worth.

Also, casino marketing linked gambling to big time entertainment long ago in the desert of Las Vegas, Nevada by offering live entertainment performances and activities. This technique will always bring people, who are potential gamblers, into casinos.

## 2.3 Bright Future

One can extrapolate from the history of gambling that gambling will exist way past our lifetime. Legalized gambling will spread until most localities in the entire free world are saturated with it. Supply and demand, rather than government regulations, will ultimately limit the boom of legalized gambling.

Casinos and government lotteries are currently the biggest and most visible gambling institutions. They should continue to be, at least for the near future, as they appeal to anyone who has the slightest inclination towards gambling. Most of them are profitable. Those that are not profitable are so only because of poor management.

Also, casinos continue to introduce new games, variations of old games, and specialized ethnic games (like pai-gow for Asians). Casino odds are usually about the same as for the old games. So, changes to games simply lure new gamblers in and previous gamblers back.

Established gambling meccas in Las Vegas and Atlantic City continue to rebuild, expand, improve services, and offer new entertainment. New casinos continue to pop up everywhere. So, there may soon be a full-fledged casino within a few hours drive for every American on the mainland.

While state lotteries have all done superb, the advent of huge multistate lotteries have only been a spark to what may become a gambling fire or fever across America. As far fetched as it may now seem, there may be even be gigantic federal and global lotteries someday.

Instead of bringing customers to gambling establishments, continuing attempts will be made to bring gambling closer to gambling customers. This will include use of cable TV and telephone, Internet, etc.. Some Internet casinos have been available, esp. Caribbean-based outfits, for a few years now. New ones are constantly popping up wherever legal. Internet casinos work well for pari-mutuel and sports betting. However, Internet casino games can be easily rigged, if desired.

One can easily sense that the prospects are good for gambling to exist as long as man roams the earth and universe. So, problem gamblers will always be confronted with a myriad of gambling opportunities. They must learn to deal with gambling by not making any more bets.

# Section Two

# Gambling and Odds

In this section, we will discuss gambling and the importance of understanding odds. Odds govern winning and losing. Even a slight edge (1%) can allow a gambling establishment to operate profitably.

# Chapter 3

# Aspects of Gambling

## 3.1 What Exactly Is Gambling?

According to Merriam Webster's Collegiate Dictionary Tenth Edition (1994):

gamble; (verb) gambled; gambling
1 a: to play a game for money or property
   b: to bet on an uncertain outcome
2: to stake something on a contingency, take a chance

gamble (noun)
1 a: an act having an element of risk
   b: something chancy
2: the playing at a game of chance for stakes

## 3.2 There Is More to Gambling

Gambling is a non-creative activity. Gambling is a non-productive activity. Gambling is entertainment with thrill of winning. Moreover, it is very expensive entertainment for problem gamblers. Gambling is a time wasting activity with the agony of defeat, when one loses.

In the 1986 movie Color of Money, Eddie Felson (in the role that Paul Newman won an Academy Award) said "Money won is twice as sweet as money earned." Winning is certainly thrilling, but losing is not.

> POINT:
>
> Money lost is twice as painful as money well spent.
>
> Money lost hurts so bad, especially if it was hard to get.

Trying to get something for nothing rarely works. Ask any problem gambler about the agony and pain he suffered and all the hours he wasted gambling and daydreaming about gambling. Look at most self-made rich people and you will find that they worked for their riches, not by gambling.

> POINT:
>
> Lottery operators, pari-mutuel betting operators, and casinos make money. So, more money is lost than won by gamblers. There are more losers than winners in gambling.

Gambling is an unbelievable destructive force, when the gambler losses more than he can afford. Problem gamblers lose a lot money, sometimes fortunes over time. Gambling losses have led to the destruction of many marriages, families, jobs/careers, and lives.

I have also witnessed strange cases in which a few gamblers seemed to gamble on purpose until they lost all of their money. It was as though they used gambling as a means to punish themselves to atone for some sins. Such individuals should find a better way to dispose of their money, such as donating their money directly to worthwhile charities and philanthropic activities (& take a tax deduction).

# Chapter 4

# Odds & the House

## 4.1 Odds

Let's examine odds. It is extremely important to do so. If one gambles and is not aware of the odds for all the bets that he makes, then he is at bigger disadvantage.

Odds are the "heart" of all gambling. Odds, advantage, edge, juice, or vig (usually between 1 to 50%) is what makes most types of gambling a winning proposition for the house or those who operate the games.

The American Gaming Commission in 1994 reported the following statistics: legalized gambling averaged $0.84 payoff on $1.00 wagered; casino payoff was 91%; horse racing payoff was 79%; and lottery payoff was 53%.

Casinos operate on the principle of gambling odds (always having a mathematical advantage) and the law of averages for the outcome of each bet accepted. Once again, in 1994, the casino payoff was .91 for every $1.00 wagered. That was 9% profit on every dollar wagered by gamblers. So, odds work for the casinos.

Also, casinos usually have more money to lose than you bring in on any given day. So, they can survive a losing streak much longer than you can. The odds are phenomenal against anyone breaking a house.

Winnings are even guaranteed for some gambling establishments. Hefty percentages of money are raked or taken out of the money pools in pari-mutuel betting and lotteries (roughly about 15% and 50%, respectively) before winnings are even distributed.

In regards to individual bets, the higher the payoff of a bet, then the higher the odds are to win & the greater the odds are to lose. Sometimes, it seems unreal when the odds of winning are reversed and interpreted as odds of losing. For example, if the odds of winning a bet are 1 in 1,000,000 (as they are in many lottery bets), then the odds of losing the same bet are 999,999 in 1,000,000.

## 4.2 The House

> POINT:
>
> One should always know who they are betting against.
>
> If you study the house and how they operate, you may
>
> never bet against them.

In pari-mutuel betting, lottery, and bingo, the gambling establishments treat gamblers like most retail businesses treat their customers. Their customary raking of the pot enable them do this.

Not only do casinos have to get you to visit them and gamble, they must also win in order to stay in business.

Alcohol is usually available (often, free). Regardless of intentions, alcohol reduces gamblers' mental ability (as in driving an automobile) to concentrate. It can also numbs feelings when gamblers lose.

POINT:

Think a lot about the house. Think about being the house and how you would win as the house.

POINT:

The house is smarter in dealing with money than the gamblers.

POINT:

If you can't beat them, join them. You can buy high grade bonds and stocks in the best managed gambling corporations (like Bally's, Circus Circus, ...).

Note that the price of any bond and stock is subject to market fluctuations and other factors. Also, the profitability of a gambling corporation depends on non-gaming activities (such as hotel, food, entertainment and other services) as well.

POINT:

By making only bets that payoff true odds, the

gambler can expect to break even (neither win nor

lose) in the long run.

# Chapter 5

# What Are the Odds

## 5.1 (Approximate) House Advantage in Odds

| | |
|---|---|
| baccarat—bank bet | 1.17% |
| baccarat—player bet | 1.63% |
| baccarat—tie | 14.1% |
| craps—pass/come bet | 1.414% |
| craps—pass/come bet with double odds | 0.61% |
| craps—pass/come bet with 5X odds | 0.32% |
| craps—pass/come bet with 10X odds | 0.18% |
| craps—don't pass/don't come bet | 1.402% |
| craps—exotic bets | 5-16.66% |
| roulette—European "Single 0" | 2.7% |
| roulette—American "Single 0" & "Double 00" | 5.26% |
| blackjack | varies widely% |
| (odds varies with many different rules and number of decks used. Odds can be 20+%, especially if the player strays from basic rules of strategy.) | |
| sic bo | 2.8-48% |
| slots/video poker | 3-20+% |

| | |
|---|---|
| poker and other card games | 5-10% |
| (5-10% of pot raked or seat rental fee) | |
| sports bet | 10% |
| (10% of winning bet) | |
| big 6 wheel | 11.1-22.2% |
| horse racing & other pari-mutuel betting | 14-25% |
| (14-25% of pot raked for operating expenses, | |
| event purses, and state & local taxes) | |
| bingo | 20+% |
| keno | 25% |
| lottery | 50+% |

## 5.2 Best Deals

It is always to the advantage of the gambler to make bets offering the best odds, as close to true odds as possible. True odds means that the payoff is exactly proportional to the real odds of winning and that nothing is taken out of the pot of money wagered. There is no advantage for the house with true odds.

The best public gambling bets are those that payoff with true odds:

a) pools in which no money is taken out. This includes friendly sporting pools, in which all money collected is returned to the participants in the form of winnings.

b) even money bets between two individuals, such as flipping a coin, choosing high or low card from a deck, picking the hand that has a hidden coin, or an equivalent deal. The odds are even to win (no edge for anyone) and there is no skill involved, just pure luck in the game.

# Chapter 6

# Games Where Skill Can Provide an Advantage

## 6.1 Casino Games

The very best skills and mastery of casino games (like baccarat, craps, blackjack, and roulette) can only enable the gambler to get the best odds allowed by the casino. Those odds are still in favor of the casino winning.

There are no systems that can lessen the mathematical advantage established by the casino in their favor. Any system that is actually a winning system is one that casinos would probably alter the game to disallow. Under certain conditions, card counting in Blackjack can be an exception.

Card counting can give the player up to a 2% edge by expecting blackjack with its 150% payoff. It is the closest thing to a winning system, but unfortunately card counting is not guaranteed to win and usually does not. The card counter must wait for the right opportunities and then, must increase the size of his/her bets many-fold in hope of a big kill. He is very fortunate if he wins. However, when the card counter fails to get blackjack and loses the huge bet, he/she ends up deep in the hole. Losing streaks happen all the time. I have played many shoes in which the casino dealer won every hand.

Furthermore, blackjack card counting is very difficult to master and execute consistently in live casinos. Otherwise, you would find everyone in casinos waiting in line for the chance to card count at the blackjack tables. Card counting is really over-publicized.

## 6.2 Sports Betting

Sports betting at casinos or with bookies is a unique form of gambling. It can take into account a gambler's up-to-the-minute knowledge of the contestants. Also, a major difference between sports betting and a casino table game (like roulette) is that a handicapper or professional odds maker (a human being) sets the initial betting odds for each bet. Final odds are set by the betting public after all bets are collected. Odds set by people's opinions are subject to human error.

Also, betting on a sports team or player that the gambler is a fan of can make the event more lively and thrilling. Winning such a sports bet can have a much more dramatic and euphoric affect on the gambler's mind than a bet on a non-sporting event. This truly makes sports gambling the liveliest action a gambler can get, but it is action that can be more addictive.

## 6.3 Other Types of Gambling

Most other types of gambling (including pari-mutuel betting and lotteries) have a pre-determined advantage to those who run the game. There are just a few exceptions, namely games involving skill. However, only the most adept can win consistently in games of skill. It is so tough for most people, it is best to forget about trying.

Furthermore, only a few individuals climb to the top pinnacle in these games and they clean out everybody else's pockets. Let's examine some of these games:

## 6.3.1 Poker and Most Other Card Games

There is significant skill and strategy involved in consistent card game winning. However, all good card players pay a substantial price (or dues) to become good. Then, most of their money is unfortunately funneled up to the top, very best players in the country and world. Even excellent players get cleaned, when they inevitably compete with the very best.

## 6.3.2 Backgammon

Backgammon tournaments can be considered as gambling events. Tournament prizes actually comes from fees and buy-ins, just like poker. This is an intriguing game of luck (with a toss a dice) and skill (knowing the best move to make in every situation).

## 6.3.3 Chess

Like backgammon, chess tournaments can also be considered as gambling events. Yet, this game is almost strictly based on skill and mastery of the game. The only luck involved are the minuscule advantage of getting to make the first move with white pieces and opponent's blunders.

## 6.3.4 Professional Sports Tournaments

Any tournaments that awards money prizes based on buy-in fees can be considered as gambling events. The most prominent of these events include billiards/pool, dart throwing, knife throwing, bowling, golf, and tennis. They involve skill, physical ability, state of fitness (at the time of competition), and often, a touch of luck (either good or bad).

## 6.4 Cheating

There can be cheating and bribery in every kind of gambling event or game. When cheating is not uncovered, it usually gives the cheaters a decided advantage.

There have been some documented incidents of fixing in horse racing and college and professional sports. Fixing or rigging an event gives the backer almost a sure thing or lock on a bet. However, the unpredictable can also happen. For example, race horses can break down or bleed, winning race horses can be disqualified, harness horses can break stride and lose too much ground, sports athletes can suffer serious injuries during the game, etc..

There have also been unverified, inconclusive rumors, and reports about cheating that occurred in nearly every other type of gambling. Even in our better regulated financial world, there have been scams with nearly every form of financial investment. Fortunately, these unlawful incidents happen very infrequently.

There are also hustlers. They first deceive victims in the degree of their ability and skill and then, take advantage of them at a latter time for a big kill. Hopefully, victims are smart enough to recognize being taken and avoid being taken twice by the same hustler.

# Chapter 7

# Financial Investments

Most financial investments in capitalistic economies are gambling instruments. Professional financial investors may disagree. However, any financial investment that can lose money as well as make money is gambling by definition. Moreover, today's day traders easily fit the mold of pari-mutuel betting gamblers.

There is a wide assortment of financial investments that money can be lost in. They include, from most risky to least risky order:

—venture capital
—futures/commodities
—stock options
—foreign investments
—junk bonds
—raw land
—individual stocks and bonds
—stock and bond mutual funds
—rental real estate

Vast fortunes can be made in these financial markets. In matter of fact, much more money can be made via these financial investments than in any of the other forms of gambling (including casino and card games, pari-mutuel betting, and number games) that have been mentioned.

There are three basic ways to earn or win money with financial investments:

a) Pick right. Great stock pickers do great research and have great instincts or intuition. They can be easily identified among the best growth stock mutual fund managers, who have consistently beaten market indexes year after year.

b) The second and third ways are related to timing. There are two schools of thought about timing. The first, is to buy and sell at the right time. Buy low and sell high.

This method works great for commodities, stock options, and individual stock picks. One must recognize when stuff is cheap and be willing to sell when it looks expensive. Successful value investors do this. They can be easily identified among the best value stock mutual fund managers, who have consistently beaten market indexes over the long term.

All of this makes sense, when market facts are considered. Commodity prices go up and down all the time. Most companies go up and down over long periods of time. Thousands of good companies have even gone out of business, over this past century.

c) The second school of thought on timing is to hold financial investments for the long term or many years, even decades. This method works great for well diversified investment portfolios. These portfolios include a balanced mix of growth and value stocks with large, mid and small cap companies; long-term, intermediate, and short-term corporate and government bond funds; international stock and bond funds, real estate, and some high risk financial investments.

Great investment companies like Fidelity, Janus, and Vanguard have many different types of mutual funds with excellent average annual returns. If you must put your money at risk, this is the best and most sound way to do it.

# Section Three

# Problem Gambling

In this section, we will analyze gamblers and the problems they face. Problem gamblers get into a vicious cycle and develop a gambling habit, that is extremely hard to break.

Review your past overall winnings and losses. Start thinking about your future and ask yourself whether gambling should be a part of it.

# Chapter 8

# Inside the Mind of Problem Gamblers

## 8.1 Intelligence

There is a saying that "Gamblers are brighter than the average person." Also, many gamblers delude themselves by thinking they are smart enough to win and win consistently. However, being smart has nothing to do with winning (except in games of skill noted in Chapter 6,6.3). Being smart may help gamblers make better bets that offer the best odds, but does not help overcome the mathematical odds against them over the long haul.

Also, gamblers do not have to be bright to gamble. There are many games for people with low IQ including lotto, keno, big six wheel, & other "numbers" games. Anyone can become a problem gambler. In matter of fact, there are problem gamblers among people of all gender, races, religious beliefs, occupations, social status, and adult age groups.

## 8.2 Why Do People Gamble?

There are many reasons why people begin gambling. Each individual has his own reasons that are directly related to his frame of mind, environment, and situation. Other reasons include the chance to win money, entertainment, challenge, excitement, past time, be like others who gamble, etc..

However, once an individual loses a substantial amount of his savings and continues to gamble, a boundary between fun and nightmare is crossed. In the case of problem gamblers, the reasons for gambling are complex and can best be described as a cycle of problem gambling.

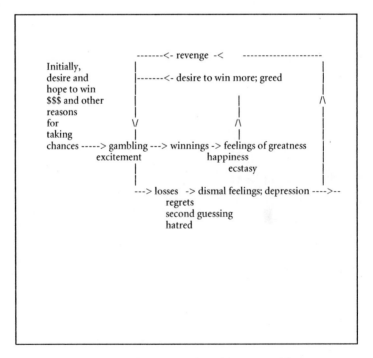

*Figure 1—The Cycle of Problem Gambling*

# 8.3 Winning

Winning is exciting and gamblers can become hooked on it. They need action. Winning actually has a drug-like effect on the mind. Almost everyone who habitually gambles had a significantly big winning day, that psyched them up into believing they were great, super, or immortal gods. They may even have bragged to relatives and friends about their accomplishment(s).

Most gamblers win occasionally and even, have some phenomenal winning streaks. However, they usually continue to gamble until their luck inevitably turns around and they become losers. Sometimes, they lose so much that they are forced to stop gambling only by needing to gather more money.

Some of these same winners go through great losses just to experience that winning, drug-like feeling again. In the long run, gambling losses usually exceed winnings. Again, mathematical odds and the law of probability for winning (with the exceptions noted in Chapter 6: Games Where Skill Can Provide An Advantage) dictate this.

# 8.4 Losing

All it usually takes is an inability to cope with losing money to get addicted to gambling. It probably would have been better for most problem gamblers to have never gambled at all. Their reasons for continuing to gamble are usually a) to try to recoup losses, b) hope or expectation for a change of luck, c) the thought that they are now smarter, wiser and know how to win, or d) simply out of habit.

However, the longer the problem gambler gambles, the more he is likely to lose. The odds are still in favor of losing with each and every bet. On Larry King Live, a brilliant and celebrated actor mentioned losing $3,000,000-, while trying to win back $2-.

The assumptions that one's losing streak must end and a winning streak is due are always wishful thinking. What usually happens is that one starts to win again and recoups some losses, but then another losing streak sets in.

Once again, losing lots of money can lead to emotional turmoil, constant regret and daydreaming, financial woes, broken families, poor job performance, job loss, and even suicide. Problem gamblers can become "victims" of gambling, very much like victims of any serious health disease.

Some gamblers run out of money and the means to get money, then commit illegal acts just to get more money to gamble with. They become criminals because of their gambling habit. At this point, they definitely have a serious problem.

Also, some overall losers continue to think of themselves as winners, based on a few big wins. However, they are simply deluded or border on delusion of being great winners. They need to first come back down to earth.

Losing continuously and heavily can adversely affect the problem gambler's entire future. He can become penniless, be left no means to support himself (including buying food and clothing), and have no security in his old age.

# Chapter 9

# Analyze Your Gambling History

## 9.1 Your Past

Do you have any idea of how much money you have lost? If you kept any records and still have them, get them out and total all of it up. If you have not kept records of your gambling winnings and losses (required for filing taxes if you had overall winnings during any calendar year), you should have. You will probably find that you have never or rarely had a winning year. For now, estimate your losses.

You will probably be shocked at how much you have really lost. It is usually much more than you think, especially if you tack on interest. If you had any winning year, there was probably some kind of a big jackpot win or extraordinary winning streak.

Also, estimate the total amount of time you spend gambling. Could you have spent that time working a part-time job, earning money and coming out way ahead?

## 9.2 Future

What will it take for you to stop gambling?
How much more must you lose, before you quit?
Do you have to lose everything that you own?

Extrapolate your potential losses through the rest of your life, if you continue gambling. Think about the rest of your life. Imagine yourself 5 or 10 years into the future, asking yourself whether it would have been better for you to have quit gambling right now (in the present time)? Also, if you now wish you never gambled at all, wisdom dictates that it is better for you to quit gambling right now.

## 9.3 Debt

In regards to borrowing unsecured money from any source, it is far more dangerous, risky, and tragic to bet with credit or money that one does not really have. There is nothing more demeaning and emotionally painful for gamblers than to gamble and lose money that they do not have. When this happens, they become devastated and awful things usually happen as a consequence.

# Section 4

# What To Do

This section reveals how a problem gambler can deal with his problem. One very important point is to set new goals.

# Chapter 10

# Solutions

## 10.1 Medicine

There is no medicine a gambler can simply take to stop him from gambling. Although, there is a current study to develop drug therapy to treat certain regions of the brain that are associated with gambling at Mount Sinai School of Medicine in New York (212-241-5287).

If a drug is ever developed to prevent one from gambling, there would be many questions as with all drugs. What percentage of patients will the drug be successful in? How effectively would the drug be for you? What and how bad will the side effects be?

However, none of this likely to come to pass. Problem gambling has never appeared to be directly caused by some physical condition or a chemical dependency (like with drugs, alcohol, and tobacco). Problem gambling is also not really caused by a mental condition or defect. For when a problem gambler occasionally wins, he exhibits no negative mental problems at all. Winning dramatically changes the problem gambler into a healthy and happy person.

The only real drug to cure a problem gambler is money. Just give him back all of the money that he lost and a new home in Hawaii. That is the instant cure for a problem gambler. Unfortunately, such a cure is too expensive.

## 10.2 An Alternative Cure

Gambling is just a game and mental activity. Recall the cycle of problem gambling that deals entirely with mental feelings. So, the solution to any gambling problem must be mental in nature.

It is now time to think and start to correct this mental problem. As obvious or simple the following points may be, the problem gambler needs to accept and believe them to the point that they affect his actions and he no longer makes a bet.

## 10.3 REALIZE the Facts about Gambling

> POINT:
>
> Acknowledge that gambling is not going away and
>
> that it is up to you to change and not gamble.

POINT:

"Gambling is fast and easy money" is a myth that drives many people to gamble. It may even seem like a fact, when you win.

However, it is a one-sided statement. The opposite side states that "Gambling is fast and easy way to lose money".

POINT:

Those who have never gambled because they recognized the probability of losing made the right decision. Those who gambled and then, gave it up also made the right decision, but had to pay a price.

POINT:

Once an individual starts gambling, he must learn the hard lessons of losing and quitting.

POINT:

A problem gambler is a loser, who continues to lose,

until he quits gambling or dies.

POINT:

Gambling can only occur, if you engage in it. So,

you really do have control over your gambling.

POINT:

You MUST accept the fact that you cannot beat

gambling over the long run. Advantages in odds,

even tiny 1% ones, will end up beating you over

time. This fact allows gambling establishments to

operate and win, year after year.

POINT:

Acknowledge what a waste of time and energy your

futile efforts at gambling have been.

POINT:

Gambling is one of the most expensive forms of

entertainment. It can be replaced by another form

of entertainment in your life for a lot less money.

POINT:

No gambling is better than reducing your gambling.

No gambling should be your ultimate goal.

POINT:

It is better to quit late in your life, than to never
quit. If you believe in life after death, you will be
better off in your next life by quitting now.
Challenge yourself to give up gambling before
you die.

POINT:

Consider the benefits of not gambling. You will not
be able to lose. By not losing, your finances will
improve in disbelief. Also, emotional turmoil and
stress associated with gambling will vanish.

POINT:

The much publicized Eastern or oriental beliefs
that gambling winnings and losses are a result of
destiny is another myth. Mathematical odds dictate
whether one wins or loose in most gambling games
over the long run.

POINT:

Easy accessibility to gambling may be important.

You can try to stay out of gambling joints and avoid

relatives and friends who go to gambling joints.

If you must enter gambling establishment(s), try to

not carry money, checks, or credit cards. If you

have credit with gambling establishment(s), you have

the right to send written request(s) to revoke or expire

your credit.

If you are on mailing list(s), you have the right to send

written requests to the marketing department(s) to

remove your name  from all direct marketing lists.

However, legal gambling is getting bigger and

bigger. It is not practical to try to run away from

gambling. Gambling opportunities will always come

your way, perhaps in the form of a lottery ticket at

the local supermarket. It is better to confront

gambling and just not make a bet.

# 10.4 Thoughts

POINT:

Admit that you are not luckily enough to win as a gambler. Admit you cannot beat gambling. Admit you are a loser. Concede to gambling.

POINT:

One of the most important points is to admit that you cannot and will not be able to win your losses back. Say bye-bye forever to all of the money that you lost. Let go of your gambling losses.

POINT:

The more tired you are of losing, the less you should gamble. When you are totally fed up with losing, you should quit gambling.

POINT:

There is no real need for any problem gambler to gamble and lose more money.

POINT:

Do not take any more chances to lose money.

POINT:

Lose the desire to gamble.

POINT:

Learn to hate losing money so much, that you won't risk losing anymore.

Repeat 40 times daily "I HATE LOSING MONEY."

10 times before breakfast

10 times before lunch

10 times before dinner

10 times before going to sleep

POINT:

Fill-in a phony $$$ bill with the total amount of

money you lost by gambling and keep it in your

wallet. (Specify at least the amount you are sure

of and add some interest, as if you saved the money

at a bank.) Use this bill as a constant reminder of

the futility of gambling to win money.

Dates __/__/__ - __/__/__

Pay to the Order of **GAMBLING LOSSES**              $__,___,___.__

_____DOLLARS

_____
Your Signature

*Figure 2—$$$ Bill Lost To Gambling*

POINT:

Set all of your past gambling losses to be your

lifetime limit for gambling losses.

POINT:

"Stop Your Gambling Losses" and you can look

forward to better life.

POINT:

If you continue to gamble, the odds favor you losing

more.

POINT:

It is better to work for your money than to fail

miserably in trying to win it.

POINT:

Visualize and dream about riches by not gambling,

but by working at any job.

POINT:

It is better to save or spend your money than to lose

it by gambling.

POINT:

If you are religious, pray every night (to your God,

inner spirit, ...) for strength to resist gambling

nightly. Even if it does not help, all you waste is

a brief moment each night, a very small price.

POINT:

Controlling a gambling habit is a test and development of character. It takes a lot of self-discipline to not gamble anymore. You can take pride in succeeding to do so.

# 10.5 Habit

POINT:

Do you gamble regularly or occasionally? If you gamble occasionally, is it because you don't have the money to gamble regularly?

It is very important to know and acknowledge whether or not you have a gambling habit? If you do, beware that habits are difficult to break.

POINT:

A gambling habit is waste of time. Gambling takes up a lot time, in daydreaming and planning, as well as while actively gambling.

POINT:

Setting new goals will help undermine your gambling habit.

POINT:

Find another place for the money that you will no longer gamble and lose. If you have any debts, pay them off first. Save for things that you always wanted to buy or accumulate wealth. Consider investing in low risk financial investments.

POINT:

Be determined to end the torment of losing money.

Bet no more and conquer your gambling habit.

---

POINT:

Overcome any fears and doubts of being a problem

gambler by not gambling.

---

POINT:

Break the vicious cycle of problem gambling now.

Do not attempt to revenge any of your losses. Let

bygones be bygones. Bet no more.

## 10.6 Mottos

Having mottos can help. Here are some:
"Don't Gamble, Save Money."
"Have a Gambling Itch. Put a salve on it."
"Say 'NO' to Gambling."
"No more bets!"
"Gambling means losing! Who wants to lose?"

## 10.7 Final Advice

POINT:

Do not promote gambling.

POINT:

Get support from your family and friends.

> POINT:
>
> Associate with those who know about gambling and
>
> do not gamble.

# 10.8 Your Thoughts

Have any other thoughts about gambling, especially ideas on how to stop your gambling? Write them here:

_____

_____

_____

_____

_____

_____

_____

_____

_____

_____

_____

_____

_____

_____

POINT:

Stay focused and centered on your goal to quit gambling.

# Chapter 11

# Goals

It is very important to define new goals for yourself. They will help you to successfully withdraw from gambling. You need to replace the time that would normally spend gambling with other active activities that are important to you and that you will enjoy doing. The activities should not be a passive ones, like watching television.

Soak up your gambling time by trying to accomplish some meaningful goals in your life. Achieving meaningful goals determine the true success of one's life. One should have goals (including morals, ideals, rules, etc.) that govern or determine his way of life.

Aim high! However, if a goal is a big lofty one, then break it into smaller ones. Make the road to achieving a huge goal a bunch of small steps, that can be more easily attained.

Work on your goals regularly. Spend at least one full hour weekly. Try to do it when you are relaxed. This will allow you to focus more clearly, better reminisce, and avoid tainting your plans. Also, add dates for reaching each your goals.

Get advice from your parents and friends. Sometimes, they know what you need better than you do. You need not follow their suggestions, but you should consider them. Also, if you announce your goals, you may get more support from others.

Goals can and should be modified when appropriate. Whenever new goals or changes come to mind, write them down before you forget.

1) Physical
  a) your health/body

_____

_____

_____

_____

_____

_____

_____

_____

  b) sports

_____

_____

_____

_____

_____

_____

_____

_____

_____

c) exercise, aerobics, dance, etc.

_____

_____

_____

_____

_____

_____

_____

_____

d) your financial situation, in terms of:

_____

_____

_____

_____

_____

_____

_____

_____

_____

_____

cash

_____

_____

_____

_____

_____

_____

_____

_____

_____

life insurance

_____

_____

_____

_____

_____

_____

_____

_____

IRA

_____

_____

_____

_____

_____

_____

_____

## 401K

_____

_____

_____

_____

_____

_____

_____

_____

_____

## Keogh

_____

_____

_____

_____

_____

_____

_____

_____

_____

_____

_____

pension

_____

_____

_____

_____

_____

_____

_____

_____

bonds

_____

_____

_____

_____

_____

_____

_____

_____

_____

_____

stocks

_____

_____

_____

_____

_____

_____

_____

_____

_____

_____

## mutual funds

_____

_____

_____

_____

_____

_____

_____

_____

## annuities

_____

_____

_____

_____

_____

_____

_____

_____

_____

_____

_____

_____

_____

_____

e) Your Home

_____

_____

_____

_____

_____

_____

_____

_____

_____

_____

f) Objects (e.g., automobiles, TV's, books, etc.)

_____

_____

_____

_____

_____

_____

_____

2) Mental

_____

_____

_____

_____

_____

_____

_____

_____

_____

_____

a) verbal skills

_____

_____

_____

_____

_____

_____

_____

b) math skills

_____

_____

_____

_____

_____

_____

_____

_____

_____

_____

c) computer skills

_____

_____

_____

_____

_____

_____

_____

_____

_____

_____

_____

_____


d) foreign language skills

_____

_____

_____

_____

_____

_____

_____

_____


e) commercial skills

_____

_____

_____

_____

_____

_____

_____

_____

_____

**f) art**

_____

_____

_____

_____

_____

_____

_____

_____

_____

_____

g) music

_____

_____

_____

_____

_____

_____

_____

_____

_____

h) trivia knowledge

_____

_____

_____

_____

_____

_____

_____

_____

_____

_____

_____

## 3) Spiritual

_____

_____

_____

_____

_____

_____

_____

_____

### a) love

_____

_____

_____

_____

_____

_____

_____

_____

_____

_____

b) faith/hope/peace

_____

_____

_____

_____

_____

_____

_____

_____

c) manners

_____

_____

_____

_____

_____

_____

_____

_____

d) giving; charity activities (money & volunteer work)

_____

_____

_____

_____

_____

_____

_____

_____

_____

_____

_____

4) Religious

_____

_____

_____

_____

_____

_____

_____

_____

5) Social

_____

_____

_____

_____

_____

_____

_____

_____

_____

_____

a) family

_____

_____

_____

_____

_____

_____

_____

_____

_____

b) friends/acquaintances

_____

_____

_____

_____

_____

_____

_____

_____

_____

c) enemies

_____

_____

_____

_____

_____

_____

_____

_____

_____

_____

_____

6) Work—list jobs that you currently have, jobs you want to have, and what you can accomplish at each job.
   job #1

_____

_____

_____

_____

_____

_____

_____

_____

_____

_____

_____

job #2

_____

_____

_____

_____

_____

_____

_____

_____

job #3

_____

_____

_____

_____

_____

_____

_____

_____

_____

_____

_____

job #4

_____

_____

_____

_____

_____

_____

_____

_____

7) Hobbies - list your current hobbies, hobbies that you are interested in, and add details (e.g., if the hobby involves a collection, define the size of the collection you want, specific pieces in the collection, etc.)

hobby #1

_____

_____

_____

_____

_____

_____

_____

_____

hobby #2

_____

_____

_____

_____

_____

_____

_____

_____

_____

_____

_____

## hobby #3

_____

_____

_____

_____

_____

_____

_____

_____

_____

## hobby #4

_____

_____

_____

_____

_____

_____

_____

_____

_____

_____

8) Miscellaneous - use this space for goals that do not fit into any of the previous categories (e.g., start a diary).

_____

_____

_____

_____

_____

_____

_____

_____

_____

# Chapter 12

# What Now

You must ACT now. Try not to gamble. Never give up trying to quit gambling. Dare to fail at trying to quit. Try, try, and try again until you succeed.

Form new habits to replace your gambling habit. Control and change your life for the better. Only you can make this become reality.

Watch out for enticements designed to lure you back. Do not give into these temptations. Also, be wary of relapses. From time to time, the gambling urge may return. Read and re-read this manual, whenever needed.

Use all of your willpower to resist betting and accomplish more in your life. Good things will follow. I truly hope this manual helps you better cope with your gambling problem and avoid some suffering. Good luck on your journey.

# Appendix

*Appendix A—DO NOT READ THIS UNLESS you have tried working with the ideas given in previous chapters and continue to gamble.*

If you have tried seriously to quit gambling and still can not break the habit, then here are some gambling tips designed to reduce losses:

1) Try to gamble without wagering any real money. Bet on paper. Write down every bet would make and keep track of what would win or lose. Keep ongoing totals. Sometimes you will miss out on winning, but more often you will save yourself from losing.
2) Learn to gamble only when you are well rested, never when you are tired. (This point deserves more attention.) When you are tired, you may make unwise decisions and take more chances. Thus, lose more.
3) Limit the amount of time that you gamble. Try to reduce the amount of time you spend gambling by 90%.
   a) Limit the number of sessions that you gamble every year. Plan the exact days during the year that you can gamble on. The fewer the days, the better. Then, try to adhere to this schedule.
   b) Shorten the amount of time that you gamble during the days you gamble. For example, if you go to a casino, gamble for only 10 or

30 minutes there. Do something else (if possible) or simply go home when time is up, whether you are winning or losing.

4) Limit the amount you bet.

    a) Make a budget for your gambling habit. Set a yearly limit for gambling. This can either be a percentage (e.g., 5% of your take home pay) or specific amount (e.g., $5,000.00). Divide your yearly limit by the number of days you plan to gamble to get a daily limit.

    b) Slow your action down by making small wagers. If your normally wager is $100, then drop it down to $25, $10 or $5. This will make your money last longer.

    c) Place reasonably small limits on BOTH the amount of money you can win as well as lose. Stop gambling for the remainder of the day once either condition is met. This prevents you from playing endlessly until you lose everything.

    d) Learn to walk away with small wins and small losses. Be willing to end a day up by a single dollar. Be willing to end a day with a small loss (like 10% of your bankroll). There is never a real need to gamble until either you win a fortune or lose everything.

5) Avoid parlay betting. When you make parlay bets (or let bets ride), "double or nothing bets", raise bets, bet everything or go for broke, in hopes of getting even or winning big, you increase the odds of losing and getting wiped out quicker.

The odds of winning a parlay even-money $2 bet are 25 % to win $8 and 75% to lose $2. The odds of winning a two separate even-money $1 bets are 25% to win $2; 50% to break-even; and 25% to lose $2. Your money lasts longer on average and you can make more bets, if you make consistent sized bets.

6) Avoid raising your bets in hope of winning back recent losses quickly. If you lose, it gets you deeper in the hole and wipes you out faster.

Never dig deeper into your pockets, especially with credit cards to try to win back money that was just lost. It is usually results in huge losses in a very short period of time.

7) Many so-called expert gamblers advise raising bets on winning streaks and lowering bets on losing streaks. When this technique works, you think you got it all figured out. Let winnings flow and minimize losses. (That is how I felt, when I used the technique in craps to score huge wins on three occasions turning $200 bankrolls into over $3,000, $7,000, and $5,000).

However, this technique simply does not work over long periods of time. In fact, it helps you to lose huge amounts in the long run. This technique depends on two things, long winning and losing streaks and timing. First, long winning and losing streaks happen far less frequently than short winning and losing streaks. This can proven by simply tossing a coin lots of time and analyzing the streaks. I tossed a coin a thousand times and got the following distribution:

| heads winning streaks | # of times | | tails losing streaks | # of times |
|---|---|---|---|---|
| 1 | 114 | | 1 | 116 |
| 2 | 60 | | 2 | 58 |
| 3 | 26 | | 3 | 26 |
| 4 | 18 | | 4 | 15 |
| 5 | 13 | | 5 | 10 |
| 6 | 3 | | 6 | 6 |
| 7 | 2 | | 7 | 3 |
| 8 | 2 | | 8 | 2 |
| 9 | 0 | | 9 | 0 |
| 10 | 0 | | 10 | 1 |

*Figure 3—Coin Toss Distribution*

Again, long winning and losing streaks happen too infrequently on average. Second, timing these streaks is impossible unless you are a genuine psychic, who can accurately foretell the outcome of gambling events consistently.

So, avoid using this technique. You will lose a lot less, in the long term, by keeping the size of your bets the same all of the time.

8) Go with games and bets giving the best odds. Become a student of "gambling odds". Study percentages for every bet. Then, bet only when you get the best deal.

While this will not help you win in the long run, mathematical probability dictates that you will do better by losing less on average. Your money will last longer.

9) Develop other rules that govern exactly when you stop gambling for the day, when you are losing. Then, live by these rules.

10) STRETCH YOUR GAMBLING DOLLARS! Here are some examples:

a) If you play casino table games, divide your bankroll into 100 bets. If you have a bankroll of $500.00, then you will have 100 $5 bets. Make the same bet 100 times consecutively and wager only basic bets. Avoid longshots or exotic bets. Again, make exactly 100 bets, no more and no less.

In craps, bet all 100 bets consecutively on either the Pass Line or Don't Pass. If you do not take any odds, the casino advantage is 1.4%. So, you can expect to lose one or two $5 bets. At a full table with 14-16 players, you can get roughly 2 or 3 hours of action.

In roulette, bet all 100 bets consecutively on either red or black (or odd or even). American Roulette payoff on these bets is .9474 cents on the dollar. The casino advantage is 5.26%. So, you can expect to lose about five $5 bets or $25. At a table with seven players, you will get about 2 hours worth of action.

b) In pari-mutuel betting, bet $6 WIN-PLACE-SHOW on the favorite in each race. In 10 events, you will wager $60 and can expect to lose roughly $10 on average and get about 4 hours of action.

Betting like this should limit and slow your losses.

11) Transform yourself from a serious gambler into a moderate gambler, and then, an occasional gambler. If you can cut your average yearly gambling losses by 25%, 50%, 75%, or 90%, you will make gradual progress towards not gambling at all.

12) Be cheap and stingy with your gambling money. Bet like a bum. Instead of gambling at places with high minimum bets, try to gamble only at places with low minimum bets.

Low bet limits imposed at Las Vegas Nights actually do good in limiting one's losses. Highrollers might still lose, but lose a lot less than at a night trip to a full-fledged casino. There are other places that have low maximum bet limits including casinos at Deadwood, South Dakota and riverboats in the Mid-west.

13) Control the amount of money that you risk losing. Do not make big bets anymore. Uncontrolled gambling is usually most destructive. It is so easy to bet big at the spur the moment (esp., with access to lots of cash) and end up with huge unrecoverable losses.

No matter what your situation, you will probably be better off by simply lowering the amount of money you gamble.

14) Of course, this is all easier said than done. The trick is to try and try and try again. Try this for a year or two, then re-read this entire manual. Repeat the process as many times as needed to eventually succeed. Better late than never.

# Appendix

## *Appendix B—Gambling Organizations*

The following organizations are of interest to problem gamblers.

American Gaming Association (a casino gaming industry
organization that lobbies Washington, DC as well as
address the issue of problem gambling)
202-637-6500
www.americangaming.org

Gam-Anon Family Groups (for families of problem gamblers)
PO Box 157
Whitestone, NY 11357
718-352-1671

Gamblers Anonymous
PO Box 17173
Los Angeles, CA 90017
213-386-8789
www.gamblersanonymous.org

National Coalition Against Legalized Gambling
800-664-2680
www.ncalg.org

National Council on Problem Gamblers
800-522-4700
www.ncpgambling.org (This website has links to little-known
state organizations.)

# Notes

Use the following space for your ideas on how to quit gambling. Be sure to jot them down as soon as possible, before forgetting them.

_____

_____

_____

_____

_____

_____

_____

_____

_____

_____

_____

_____

_____

_____

_____

_____

# Index

# References

1www.usatoday.com, on-line news for April 5, 1999

2Encyclopedia Americana, 1993 Edition

3Encyclopedia Americana, 1993 Edition

4USA Weekend, 9/20-22/91

5USA Weekend, 2/10-12/95

6Poughkeepsie Journal, 8/20/95

7Poughkeepsie Journal, 5/30/99

Printed in the United States
25651LVS00004B/417